Molière's DON JUAN

also by Christopher Hampton

MOLIERE'S

DON JUAN

translated by

CHRISTOPHER HAMPTON

FABER AND FABER
3 Queen Square
London

First published in 1974
by Faber and Faber Limited
3 Queen Square London WC1
Printed in Great Britain by
Whitstable Litho

ISBN   0 571 10193 3

All rights whatsoever in this play are
strictly reserved and applications for
permission to perform it, etc., must be
made in advance, before rehearsals
begin, to Margaret Ramsay Ltd.,
14a Goodwin's Court, St. Martin's Lane,
London W.C.2.

CONDITIONS OF SALE

For
Merlin

CHARACTERS

DON JUAN, Don Louis' son
SGANARELLE, Don Juan's valet
ELVIRA, Don Juan's wife
GUZMAN, Elvira's squire
DON CARLOS
DON ALONSO   Elvira's brothers
DON LOUIS, Don Juan's father
CHARLOTTE
MATHURINE   peasants
PIERROT
THE STATUE of the Commander
LA VIOLETTE   Don Juan's servants
RAGOTIN
MR. DIMANCHE, a tradesman
LA RAMEE, a swordsman
A BEGGAR
A GHOST

Followers of Don Juan, Don Carlos, Don Alonso, etc.

The scene is some port in Sicily, possibly Palermo.

ristopher Hampton's translation of Molière's <u>Don Juan</u>
s commissioned by BBC Radio 3 and transmitted on
1 January 1972. The cast was as follows:

N JUAN	Kenneth Haigh
ANARELLE	Bill Fraser
VIRA	Sheila Grant
ZMAN	Patrick Tull
N CARLOS	David Bailie
N ALONSO	John Rye
N LOUIS	Rolf Lefebvre
ARLOTTE	Kate Binchy
ATHURINE	Penelope Lee
ERROT	Brian Hewlett
E STATUE OF THE COMMANDER	Geoffrey Wincott
VIOLETTE	David Timson
R. DIMANCHE	James Thomason
RAMEE	Patrick Tull
BEGGAR	Leslie Heritage
GHOST	Penelope Lee

oduced by John Tydeman

A stage production was mounted at the Bristol Old Vic on 24th May, 1972. The cast was as follows:

DON JUAN	Tom Baker
SGANARELLE	John Nettles
ELVIRA	Helen Christie
GUZMAN	Patrick Monckton
DON CARLOS	Ronald Magill
DON ALONSO	Patrick Monckton
DON LOUIS	Paul Imbusch
CHARLOTTE	Emma Jean Richard
MATHURINE	Hazel Clyne
PIERROT	Ian Gelder
THE STATUE OF THE COMMANDER	Roger Forbes
LA VIOLETTE	Hazel Clyne
MR. DIMANCHE	John Parker
A BEGGAR	John Parker

Directed by David Phethean
Designed by Alex Day
Lighting by Jeremy Godden

A Note on the Translation

e purpose of this translation (and it is a translation
the play, rather than the kind of adaptation Brecht
de of Don Juan for the Berliner Ensemble) is simply
provide a clear, fluent and easily speakable version
the play, amusing where necessary, and written, as
elieve the original must have been, very much with
ors and audiences in mind. To this end, I have oc-
sionally sacrificed accuracy for grace, and made
ne minor omissions in Act III, Scenes 3 and 4, Act
, Scenes 4 and 6 and Act V, Scene I, wherever I
t the weighty hand of the Spanish original, with its
roque concepts of honour and florid moralising,
ng too heavily across Molière's sprightly prose.
t those who know the play well should not, I hope,
d this version too distant, in spirit or in detail,
m the original play.

FOREWORD

olière wrote <u>Don Juan</u>, rather hastily at the end of
54, to fill in the unforeseen gap in his programme
used by the banning of the first (and now lost) ver-
on of <u>Tartuffe</u>. Although written when Molière was
the height of his powers (between <u>Tartuffe</u> and <u>Le</u>
<u>santhrope</u>), the play, despite an immediate success
the box office, was withdrawn after only fifteen per-
rmances, presumably as a result of political pres-
re, and fell at once into the deepest obscurity, from
ich it has emerged only in the last twenty-five years,
ring which time it has become one of the most popu-
r plays in the Molière repertoire. After the first
oduction it remained unperformed until 1841, and
ereafter very rarely performed until the famous
avet production of 1947 - and in fact, were it not for
oreign edition printed in Amsterdam in 1683, the
mplete text would not have survived at all, as those
ements of the play (such as the scene with the Beg-
r and a number of Sganarelle's more buffoonish de-
nces of conventional morality) deemed to be most
ensive were bowdlerized when the first official
ition of Molière's complete works was published in
ance.

Of all Molière's plays, why should this most

bizarre and unusual piece have been so decisively adopted by the twentieth century? The simple answer is that those qualities which condemned the play in the eyes of Molière's contemporaries - its subversiveness, its ambiguities and its disquieting variety of styles - are precisely the qualities which commend it to modern audiences, accustomed as they are, through the work of certain modern playwrights, to the mixture of knock-about farce and metaphysical speculation which runs through Don Juan. This, however, is not really an adequate explanation of the play's continuing appeal: especially if we take into account the fact that what was most shocking to a seventeenth century audience - Don Juan's defiant attitude towards conventional religion - scarcely raises an eyebrow today and indeed can only really be accepted as a familiar and inevitable feature of the Don Juan legend. To my mind, the real force of the play lies in another, more specific area: it lies in the nature of the relationship between the two principal characters.

As soon as he appears, Don Juan gives us the key to his character: curiosity. Jacques Guicharnaud, in a long essay on the play (in Molière: une aventure théâtrale, Editions Gallimard, 1963), from which I have borrowed or adapted a number of ideas, points out that Don Juan's first eight speeches are all questions, while his first long speech describes how he has devoted himself with single-minded intensity to the satisfying of his curiosity. His life is a mathematical progression of sexual conquest so all-embracing that it enables him to reduce all existence to a basic
16

mula: "I believe that two and two are four,
anarelle, and that four and four are eight." The
ncipal theatrical device Molière uses to underline
 overriding nature of this obsession is the perver-
n of language. For Don Juan, language is only se-
darily a means of communication: its first use is as
eapon, increasingly a defensive weapon as the play
ceeds from the arrogant sarcasm with which he
ets Elvira in the first act and the poetic schemati-
ion of his methods of seduction in Act II, to the pru-
t hypocrisy of the last act. And if language is a
apon for Don Juan, silence is a shield. "Oh, for
d's sake, come on, interrupt me." Sganarelle is
e forced to protest, "You're not saying anything
purpose, it's very cruel, just letting me rattle on
e that." - and on more serious occasions than this
n Juan turns himself into a vacuum. One senses the
wing uneasiness in the debate between Don Carlos
l Don Alonso (Act III, Scene 4), as its object looks
lly and silently on, and the same effect dominates
 scenes in Act IV, in which Don Juan is confronted
st by his father and then by Elvira.
 Words are meaningless to Don Juan because they
not touch his body, and he is a man for whom only
 physical world exists. It is physical barriers
ich upset his plans - the storm which capsizes his
t, the arrival of Pierrot, the arrival of Mathurine,
 arrival of his pursuers. Finally, his punishment
 only be physical. Molière sums all this up in one
mbol: in the cogent, ordered fourth act he shows us
oncentrated reprise of all the moral pressures on
n Juan, who is reminded one after another of his
igations towards his creditors, his parents, his

17

forsaken lovers, and finally towards God. But his only response to this is an increasingly urgent demand for the satisfaction of his body:

"I want dinner now, as soon as possible."

"How much longer is dinner going to be?"

"Hurry up with the dinner."

Like the Commander who then appears, Don Juan is flesh made stone.

Molière shows us this clearly, but not too clearly. Although Don Juan is demonstrably selfish, perverse and totally unscrupulous, the play contains enough incident to tempt the unwary into sympathy for him. He shows generosity (albeit tinged with sadism) to a beggar, giving him money "for the love of humanity." He shows courage in defending a stranger against robbers (albeit of a familiarly mathematical kind: "Three against one?"). He shows elegance and wit throughout, particularly in the dismissal of his creditor, M. Dimanche. But all these are the virtues, or if not the virtues, the prerogatives of privilege. The actor playing Don Juan should set himself a task: to seduce the audience. He should fail, but he probably won't. If he succeeds, it might be noted that this will be his only successful seduction of the play.

Except perhaps for his seduction of Sganarelle, this is the part which Molière chose to play himself, and, as I need hardly point out, Molière was no fool. Like Arnolphe (in L'École des Femmes) and Orgon (in Tartuffe) - two other Molière roles - Sganarelle belongs to that group of Molière characters who, by virtue of a certain shallow cynicism, labour under the misap-

ehension that they are sophisticated men of the
rld. When Sganarelle describes his master as "the
eatest criminal the world has ever seen", his admi-
:ion, his envy and even his pride are transparent.
reads Don Juan the way some people read porno-
aphy - with the fascinated disapproval of the pru-
ent.

Sganarelle represents the negative qualities of
tue, as Don Juan represents the positive qualities
vice. If he speaks up on behalf of Don Juan's vic-
s, it is more from a wish for peace and quiet than
m genuine compassion. If he urges the claims of
tue and religion, he does so out of laziness and ig-
cance. He may, as many critics suggest, be Every-
n, but he is a sour and uncompromising portrait of
eryman, and we may note that his attempt to prove that
ere's some wonderful quality in man" leads only to
s ignominious collapse. Molière uses him to show us
e gradual breakdown of logic caused by the anarchy
Don Juan: in the first act his condemnation of Don Juan's
haviour has coherence and even a certain sophistication;
the third act Don Juan's silence begins to fracture his
gic; and by the last act, his final appeal to Don Juan is
mplete gibberish, the conclusion of which ("you're going
be damned right to Hell") is true, even though the
ain of reasoning has been reduced by the complete
ogic of human motives to incoherent and random word-
sociation. As Guicharnaud says, Sganarelle is the risk
run if we condemn Don Juan. He is the inefficient re-
esentative of reason, the impotent spokesman of com-
table morality, the accomplice in us all.

19

The harsh moral of this rigorous fable rings as true
today as it ever has: if you let yourself be fucked, you
will be. This is not a comforting play. The hero, as
so often in Molière, is in the grip of an obsession, and
the further away from mere eccentricity the obsession
is, the more serious the comedy becomes. Here, dea-
ling with the most basic of all human urges, Molière
explores the furthest boundaries of comedy. And as
the play ends, he achieves a balance by a skilful ma-
nipulation of the rasp of conflicting styles. Sganarelle's cry for his wages bludgeons laughter from the
audience, and sums up in one word the ironies and
conclusions of the play, the bleak information that
while no-one gets the wages he anticipates, everyone
gets the wages he deserves. No insoluble problems
have been solved and Molière's sense of scale is im-
peccable: for as a result of the intervention of God,
Don Juan will languish for ever in the vaults of Hell -
and Sganarelle will be unable to afford his tobacco.

CHRISTOPHER HAMPTON

ACT ONE

SCENE ONE

SGANARELLE, GUZMAN

ANARELLE: (holding a tobacco-pouch) Whatever
Aristotle and the Philosophers may say, there's
nothing like tobacco: the most respectable men have
a passion for it, and if you don't like it, what's the
point of living, I say. You see, it not only cheers
you up and clears your brain out, it actually teaches
you how to be virtuous and ... respectable.
Haven't you noticed how well people behave as soon
as they start taking it, how pleased they are to offer
it round, wherever they are? They never wait to be
asked, you see, because tobacco makes you so
honourable and ... virtuous that you anticipate
people's wishes. Yes. Now, what were we talking
about? Ah yes, Donna Elvira. You were saying, my
dear Guzman, that she was surprised when we left,
which is why she's set off after us, right? And that
my master has affected her soul so deeply, correct
me if I'm wrong, that she would have died if she
hadn't come here to find him. Well. Between you and
me, if you want my opinion, I think she's in trouble.
I'm afraid her trip was rather pointless. I think
she'd have done better to say at home.

ZMAN: Why? Tell me, Sganarelle, what makes you so
pessimistic? Has your master said anything to you

about it, I mean did he leave because he was annoy
with us or something?

SGANARELLE: No, no. But I can more or less tell the
way things are going. He hasn't said anything to me
about it yet, but I bet I know what the situation is.
Of course, it's possible I'm mistaken; but with my
experience, I do have some insight into these matte

GUZMAN: Are you implying Don Juan is unfaithful? Is h
capable of betraying Donna Elvira's love?

SGANARELLE: Well, he's a young man ...

GUZMAN: How could he do a thing like that? He's an
aristocrat.

SGANARELLE: What's that got to do with it?

GUZMAN: But he's bound by the ... er ... bonds of ho
matrimony.

SGANARELLE: My poor Guzman, believe me, you've
got no idea what sort of a man Don Juan is.

GUZMAN: You're right, I've got no idea what sort of a
man he could be, if he behaves like that. After all
those sighs and promises and passionate letters. It
wasn't easy to persuade her to leave the convent,
you know. I really don't understand it.

SGANARELLE: You wouldn't find it difficult to understand if you knew him like I do. I'm not saying he's
changed his mind about Donna Elvira, I've no proof
of it: as you know, he sent me on here before he
left, and I haven't spoken to him since he arrived;
but I do think I ought to warn you, entre nous, that
Don Juan is the greatest criminal the world has eve
seen - a lunatic, an animal, a devil, a Turk and a
heretic. He doesn't believe in either Heaven or Hel
He doesn't even believe in werewolves. He behaves
like a brute beast, he's an Epicurean pig, he

22

doesn't take a blind bit of notice of anything you say
to him, and he makes a mockery of everything we
believe in. He may have married Donna Elvira, but
I assure you he would have done much more than that
to get what he wanted, he would have married her,
her dog, her cat, and you as well. In fact, marriage
is his favourite ploy, he's a compulsive husband.
No one is too hot or too cold for him; and if I were
to tell you the names of all the women he's married
at one time or another, we'd be here all day and
half the night as well. What are you blushing for?
That's only a broad outline. You wait till I get to the
details. He'll be struck down one day, I tell you; I'd
be better off working for the Devil than for him.
He's shown me so many disgusting things ... I don't
like to say where I wish him. There's nothing
worse than an aristocrat with no morals ... You see,
I've got to obey him, whatever my feelings are: I do
my job well because I'm a coward - but it means that
I'm forced to applaud what I secretly hate. Oh, there
he is, look, walking on the terrace: let's separate.
Just a minute, listen, I've been very frank with you,
in fact I got a bit carried away, but if any of it gets
back to his ears, I'll tell him you're a liar.

SCENE TWO

DON JUAN, SGANARELLE

DON JUAN: Who was that? He looked not unlike the wor
   Guzman.

SGANARELLE: Not unlike him.

DON JUAN: Was it?

SGANARELLE: Yes.

DON JUAN: How long has he been here?

SGANARELLE: Since yesterday evening.

DON JUAN: What's he doing?

SGANARELLE: I imagine you wouldn't have much troub
   guessing what his problem is.

DON JUAN: Our disappearance?

SGANARELLE: Yes, he's a bit upset about it. He
   wanted to know the reason for it.

DON JUAN: And did you tell him?

SGANARELLE: I said you hadn't spoken to me about it.

DON JUAN: But you must have a theory. What's your
   assessment of the situation?

SGANARELLE: Well, I wouldn't like to offend you ...
   but I'd guess you were in love.

DON JUAN: Would you?

SGANARELLE: Yes.

DON JUAN: Right. You're right. I have to admit that
   another woman has driven Donna Elvira from my
   thoughts.

SGANARELLE: See, I know you like the back of my
   hand. I know you have to live your life on tour-
   moving, as it were, from engagement to engagement

DON JUAN: And don't you think I'm right to live like tha

SGANARELLE: Sir ...

DON JUAN: Well. Tell me.

24

GANARELLE: Of course you're right if you want to.
Nobody's denying that. But if you didn't want to, it
might be a different matter.

DN JUAN: Come on, tell me what you think about it.
I give you permission to say what you like.

GANARELLE: Well then in that case, sir, quite
frankly, I must say that I strongly disapprove of
your behaviour. I think it's wicked to go round like
you do, falling in love all over the place.

DN JUAN: Do you really think I should restrict myself
to the first woman I come across, do you think I
should give up the world for her and never look at
anyone else? I suppose you think it's wonderful, all
this fake pride people take in being faithful, in
burying themselves for ever in one meaningful
relationship and in being dead from their youth on to
all the beautiful women they might meet. No. Fidelity
is for fools; if a woman is beautiful, she has a right
to my attention. Why should the fact I met someone
else first ruin her chances? Beauty delights me
wherever I find it; it has a pleasantly violent effect,
which I always give in to. What does it matter if I'm
married? Just because I'm in love with someone,
doesn't mean I should be unfair to everyone else. I
have a connoisseur's eye, I judge each case on its
merits and distribute the appropriate rewards. I can
refuse nothing to a pretty face. And the excitement of
a fresh desire - I can't explain it but for me all the
pleasure of love is in variety. You choose a beautiful
young girl, you soften her heart with judicious
flattery, you watch your own slow but daily progress,
you use eloquence and sighs and tears to attack her
innocence and inhibitions, you break down all her

little scruples one by one, you overcome the morals she's so proud of, and gently lead her to the destination - it's a marvellous process. But once you've arrived, what else is there? There's nothing left to hope for. All the beauty has gone out of the relationship, and if it wasn't for some other woman reawakening your desire by showing you a new set of attractions, you'd sink into a bog of sleepy tranquillity. I'm as ambitious as a general who advances continually from victory to victory, because he can't bear to limit his desires - nothing matches the sense of achievement I have when I make a beautiful woman give way, and nothing will stop me pursuing that achievement. I know I could make love to the whole world; and like Alexander the Great, I wish there were other worlds, so I could visit them and make new conquests.

SGANARELLE: My God, you can talk! That sounded like a prepared speech.

DON JUAN: Have you anything to say against it?

SGANARELLE: Yes. What I've got to say is ... I don't know what to say. The way you put things, you always seem to be right; and yet it's quite obvious that you're not. I had a number of unanswerable points to make, but I've forgotten them now. Never mind - next time I have an argument with you, I'll write it all down in advance.

DON JUAN: You'd be wise to.

SGANARELLE: In view of the fact you asked my opinion, I hope it wouldn't be overstepping the mark if I said I was a tiny bit shocked by your way of life.

DON JUAN: What way of life?

SGANARELLE: Oh, it's very good of its kind. It's just

the odd thing like you getting married every month.

ON JUAN: I like getting married.

ANARELLE: Oh, yes, I agree, it's very nice, yes, great fun, and I wouldn't mind at all ... but I mean, you know, it is a holy sacrament.

ON JUAN: That is a matter between God and myself, which we can work out perfectly satisfactorily, without you bothering yourself about it.

ANARELLE: I've always been told that it's dangerous to make jokes about God, and that atheists never come to any good.

ON JUAN: I've told you before, idiot, I don't like moralizing.

ANARELLE: Oh, I wasn't talking to you, sir, God forbid! You know what you're doing, and if you don't believe in anything, you have your reasons. But there are some little upstarts in this world, who've got no idea why they're atheists, except that they think it suits them to be outspoken. And if I worked for someone like that, I'd look him straight in the eye, frankly, and say to him: "How dare you make fun of Heaven, how can you bring yourself to turn the most sacred subjects into a joke without fear of damnation. I suppose you think, you ant, you earthworm (I'd say to him) that you're entitled to mock what everyone else respects. Just because you're an aristocrat with a fashionable wig, feathers in your hat, gold on your clothes and orange ribbons (I don't mean you, I mean this other man) it doesn't make you any cleverer, does it, doesn't mean you can do exactly what you like or that nobody will dare to tell you what they think of you? I'm only your servant, but I'm telling you that sooner or later God punishes sinners, a bad life comes to a bad end, and ..."

DON JUAN: That's enough!

SGANARELLE: Now what?

DON JUAN: Now we must concentrate on a beautiful girl I've fallen for and followed to this town.

SGANARELLE: Aren't you worried about the Commander you killed here six months ago?

DON JUAN: Why should I be? I killed him properly didn't I?

SGANARELLE: Very properly. I'm sure he'd have no complaints about that.

DON JUAN: I was acquitted.

SGANARELLE: Oh, yes, you were acquitted. But I don't think his friends and relations were very happy about it.

DON JUAN: Let's not think about all these disagreeable things, let's just think of pleasure. She's very lovely, you know, this girl I was telling you about, she's been brought here by her fiancé. I happened to see them three or four days before they left. I've never seen two people look happier together, or more obviously in love with each other. I was ... moved by their tenderness, it was so demonstrative My love grew from jealousy. I couldn't bear to see them so happy, it got more and more frustrating, and I thought how satisfying it would be to damage their relationship, and destroy their attachment, which offends my sensibilities. However, so far all my efforts have failed so I shall have to resort to my emergency plan. Today he's arranged to treat her to a boat trip. I haven't told you anything about this yet, but I've made all the preparations, I've hired a boat and some men, and I shall have no difficulty whatsoever in kidnapping her.

ANARELLE: But, sir ...

N JUAN: Yes?

ANARELLE: Nothing, you're quite right, it's an
excellent plan. There's nothing like doing what you
want to.

N JUAN: Right, get ready to come with me, and make
sure you bring all my weapons, in case ...
(He sees DONNA ELVIRA.)
God, it's her! You oaf, you didn't tell me she was
here.

ANARELLE: You didn't ask me.

N JUAN: What is she wearing? She must be mad, she
looks terrible.

SCENE THREE

ELVIRA, DON JUAN, SGANARELLE

VIRA: Would you be kind enough to acknowledge me,
Don Juan? Would you mind looking at me, or is that
too much to hope for?

N JUAN: You surprise me, madam, I must confess. I
wasn't expecting to see you here.

VIRA: I can see that. And I can see that you aren't
pleasantly surprised. Your reaction confirms what
up to now I've refused to believe. I'm amazed I
could have been stupid enough to doubt what's been
obvious for so long. I wanted to deceive myself.
I found reasons to account for the change in your
attitude, and I made up all kinds of plausible excuses
to explain to myself why you'd left so suddenly,
rather than accepting the truth. But the way you

29

looked at me when you first saw me told me much
more than I ever wanted to admit. I have no more
doubts: but I would like to hear you explain why yo
left me. Tell me, I want to see how you justify
yourself.

DON JUAN: Sganarelle knows why I left. He'll explain.

ELVIRA: All right. Tell me, Sganarelle. It doesn't
matter who tells me.

DON JUAN: (beckoning SGANARELLE to approach) Co
on, speak to the lady.

SGANARELLE: What do you want me to say?

ELVIRA: Come here, if that's the way he wants it. Tel
me why you left so suddenly.

DON JUAN: Answer.

SGANARELLE: Answer what? You're making fun of me

DON JUAN: Will you answer?

SGANARELLE: Madam ...

ELVIRA: What?

SGANARELLE: Sir ...

DON JUAN: (threatening him) Look ...

SGANARELLE: Madam, we had to leave because of
Alexander the Great, the generals and the other
worlds. Will that do, sir?

ELVIRA: Would you mind enlarging on that, Don Juan?

DON JUAN: To tell the truth ...

ELVIRA: Have you no idea how to defend yourself? You
ought to be used to these situations. Your confusio
is quite pathetic. You might at least manage a certa
stylish insolence. Why don't you swear to me that
you still feel the same about me, that you love me
passionately and that only death will separate us?
Why don't you tell me you were summoned away to
deal with matters of the most extreme urgency, ask

me to return home and say you'll follow me as soon
as possible, say you can't wait to get back, say
that without me you're like a body without a soul.
You might make an effort, instead of all this
embarrassment.

N JUAN: I admit I have no talent for pretence, I've
always been a sincere man. I can't say I feel the
same about you or that I can't wait to get back to
you, when I know that I only left to get away from
you: not for the reasons you imagine, but because of
my conscience, because I felt I could no longer live
with you without committing a mortal sin. I reflected
that to marry you, I had abducted you from the
convent, that you had broken the most solemn vows,
and that God is very particular about that sort of
thing. I repented, you see, I feared the wrath of
heaven; our marriage, it seemed to me, was nothing
but disguised adultery, which would result in
some terrible celestial punishment, so I decided I
would have to try to forget you, and let you return
to your previous engagement. Madam, how could you
oppose such a sacred thought, how could you expect
me to keep you and defy God, how ...?

VIRA: Now I know what sort of a criminal you are.
And it's too late for it to do anything but make things
worse. But you won't get away with it, you may
mock God, but He'll punish you for what you've done
to me.

N JUAN: Ah, Sganarelle, God ...

ANARELLE: Yes, we try not to bother about things
like that.

N JUAN: Madam ...

VIRA: That's quite enough. I don't want to hear any

more, I've heard too much already. Don't expect me to start complaining and insulting you, I'm not going to waste my time talking, I prefer to devote my energy to revenge.

(Exit ELVIRA.)

SGANARELLE: No conscience at all.

DON JUAN: (after a moment's thought) Right, I'm in lov Come on, we've got work to do.

SGANARELLE: (alone) He's a terrible man.

ACT TWO

SCENE ONE

PIERROT, CHARLOTTE

ARLOTTE: That was a bit of luck then, Pierrot, wasn't it?

ERROT: A right close shave, if you ask me. Another minute and they'd both have drowned.

ARLOTTE: Was it that gale this morning made them capsize?

ERROT: I'll tell you the whole story, Charlotte, shall I, just as it happened; because you might say I was the first to see them, I mean, what I mean is, I saw them first. I was down by the sea with fat Lucas, having a bit of a laugh, fooling about with these lumps of earth, throwing them at him, trying to hit his head, because, you know, he's fond of a laugh, is old Lucas, and I like a laugh now and then as well. Anyway, there we were, having a laugh, laughing, when I saw something bobbing about in the water, miles away it was, but it kept getting nearer. I looked at it for a minute, and suddenly I saw that I couldn't see anything any more. "Here, Lucas," I said, "I think there's some men swimming out there." "There's something wrong with your eyes," he said, "you've been eating too many carrots." "Carrots," I said, "what you talking about, carrots?" I said. "There's nothing wrong with my eyes, those are

33

men out there." "It's a mirage," he said. "Want a bet," I said, "it's not a mirage," I said, "it's two men," I said, "swimming this way," I said. "All right," he said, "I bet you it's not." "Right," I said, "bet you half-a-dollar it is." "Done," he said. "Here's my money," he said. I'm no fool you know. Quick as a flash, quick as downing a pint, I put down half-a-dollar in pennies; because I don't mind taking a chance, you know, I'm pretty daring when it comes to it. Not that I didn't know what I w doing. I'm not stupid. Anyway. no sooner had we placed our bets, when we saw these two blokes qui clearly, waving at us for help. So I grabbed the stakes and said: "Come on, Lucas, it's us they're shouting at, let's go and give them a hand." "No, why should I?" he said, "They cost me money." Anyway, to cut a long story short, I went on at him for a bit, and we got a boat, rowed out to them, pulled them out the water, took them home, and the took all their clothes off and dried themselves in front of the fire. Then two more of the same crew turned up, who'd got ashore by themselves, and finally Mathurine arrived, and one of them couldn't keep his eyes off her. There you are, Charlotte, that's what happened.

CHARLOTTE: Pierrot, didn't you say one of them was better looking than the others?

PIERROT: Yes, the man in charge. He must be a very, very important man, his clothes are covered with gold: and even his servants are pretty posh. Still, doesn't matter how important he is, he would have drowned if I hadn't been there.

CHARLOTTE: Get on!

PIERROT: He would! If it wasn't for us he'd be six
   foot under.

CHARLOTTE: Is he still at your place with no clothes
   on?

PIERROT: No, no, we watched them getting dressed.
   God. I've never seen anything like it. What a panto-
   mime! I know I'd get lost in that lot, it's quite
   amazing. Did you know they had hair, nothing to do
   with their heads, that they put on at the end like a
   big linen hat? And I tell you, you and I could both
   fit in their shirt-sleeves, no trouble at all. Instead
   of britches, they got a sort of wide apron, stretching
   from here to January. Then they got these little
   waistcoats instead of doublets, that don't even
   come down as far as their belly. Instead of neck-
   bands, they have a great big neckerchief with four
   white tassels hanging down to their stomach. Then
   they got frills on their sleeves, and these great big
   lace things on their legs - and on top of all that,
   they're covered with ribbons, you can hardly see
   them for ribbons, it's disgusting. They've even got
   them all over their shoes. I'm glad I don't have to
   wear them. I'd keep falling over them if I did.

CHARLOTTE: Oh, Pierrot, I must go and have a look.

PIERROT: Just a minute, Charlotte. I got something I
   want to say to you first.

CHARLOTTE: What?

PIERROT: Well, Charlotte, see, the time has come, as
   they say, to open my heart and get it off my chest. I
   love you, you know that, and I'm all for us getting
   married; but look, I'm not pleased with you, you
   know, I'm not.

CHARLOTTE: What do you mean? Why not?

PIERROT: Well ... well, I'll be frank with you. You
upset me.

CHARLOTTE: How?

PIERROT: It's just that you don't love me.

CHARLOTTE: Is that all?

PIERROT: What do you mean, is that all, it's enough,
isn't it?

CHARLOTTE: Honestly, Pierrot, you always say the
same thing.

PIERROT: I always say the same thing, because it alwa
is the same thing. If it wasn't always the same thin
I wouldn't always say the same thing.

CHARLOTTE: But what's the matter? What do you want

PIERROT: I want you to love me.

CHARLOTTE: I do love you, don't I?

PIERROT: No, you don't. I do my best, you know. Eve
pedlar I see, I buy you a ribbon, and do I ever com
plain? I break my neck getting you blackbirds' nest
I always get the fiddler to play for you on your
birthday. I might just as well be running my head
against a brick wall. It's not right, you know, not
loving people that love you.

CHARLOTTE: But I do love you.

PIERROT: Nice way to love someone!

CHARLOTTE: Well, what do you want me to do?

PIERROT: I just want you to behave like somebody in
love.

CHARLOTTE: I do, don't I?

PIERROT: No. If you really love someone, it shows, yo
know, it shows in the way you treat them. I mean,
look at that fat girl, Thomasina. She's potty about
that Robin. She's always hanging round him, gettin
up his nose, she never gives him a minute's peace.

She's always playing tricks on him and flicking his
ears and that. The other day he was about to sit
down on a stool, and she whipped it away and laid
him out. That's love, you see, that's how you can
tell. Not like you, you hardly ever speak to me, you
got about as much conversation as a lump of wood. I
could meet you twenty times a day, without you even
noticing me, let alone talking to me. It's not good
enough, it isn't, you're too cold.

CHARLOTTE: What can I do about it? It's my nature,
  isn't it, I can't help that.

PIERROT: Your nature's nothing to do with it. If people
  like someone, they always show it somehow or other.

CHARLOTTE: Listen, I love you as much as I can, and
  if you don't like it, you must go and find someone
  else.

PIERROT: That's exactly what I mean. You wouldn't
  say that if you loved me.

CHARLOTTE: You do go on.

PIERROT: No, look don't get angry. All I want is for you
  to be a bit more friendly.

CHARLOTTE: All right, then, all right, don't nag on
  about it. Perhaps it'll just happen one day out of
  the blue.

PIERROT: All right, Charlotte, let's shake on it.

CHARLOTTE: There you are.

PIERROT: Promise me you'll try and love me more.

CHARLOTTE: I'll do my best, but it's supposed to
  just happen, you know. Is that that gentleman?

PIERROT: That's the one.

CHARLOTTE: Ooh, he's smashing, isn't he, I'm glad he
  wasn't drowned.

PIERROT: I'll be back in a minute; I'm just going for

a quick pint, I feel a bit tired after all that
exercise.

SCENE TWO

DON JUAN, SGANARELLE, CHARLOTTE

DON JUAN: We slipped up, Sganarelle. Our careful pla
completely ruined by a sudden gale. Still, that girl
I've just left has more than made up for it, she's
charming enough to make me forget all the irritation
our failure caused me. I mustn't let that one get
away. Actually, judging by the work I've put in
already, I don't think she'll be detaining me much
longer.

SGANARELLE: You amaze me, sir, I must admit. We'v
just narrowly escaped drowning. You ought to be
thanking God for His mercy. Not going straight bac
to work, making Him angry again with your usual
lech ...
(DON JUAN begins to look threatening.)
I'm a complete fool, I don't know what I'm talking
about, you know exactly what you're doing. Sorry
I spoke.

DON JUAN: (seeing CHARLOTTE) Ah, what have we
here, Sganarelle? Have you ever seen anything
prettier? She's as good as the other one, isn't she,
don't you think?

SGANARELLE: Oh, definitely. Take your partners.

DON JUAN: (to CHARLOTTE) What a delightfully un-
expected meeting. Do you mean to tell me there

are people like you to be found in these backwoods?

CHARLOTTE: Yes. Sir.

DON JUAN: Are you from the village?

CHARLOTTE: Yes, Sir.

DON JUAN: Do you live there?

CHARLOTTE: Yes, Sir.

DON JUAN: What's your name?

CHARLOTTE: Charlotte, Sir, at your service.

DON JUAN: Isn't she beautiful? Her eyes are so piercing.

CHARLOTTE: Sir, you're embarrassing me.

DON JUAN: You shouldn't be embarrassed by the truth.
What do you think, Sganarelle? Can you imagine
anything more delightful? Just turn round, will you?
Perfect figure. Lift your head a bit, if you don't
mind. Very pretty face. Open your eyes wide.
They're beautiful. Now let's see your teeth, if I
may. Charming, and your lips look so tempting. I'm
delighted. I've never seen anyone so lovely.

CHARLOTTE: That's all very well, sir, but for all I
know, you're just making fun of me.

DON JUAN: Making fun of you? How could I, I'm in love
with you, I've never been more sincere in my life.

CHARLOTTE: Well, if you mean that, thank you very
much.

DON JUAN: Not at all, don't thank me, it's your beauty
you should thank.

CHARLOTTE: Sir, you're confusing me, I don't know
what to say.

DON JUAN: Sganarelle, look at her hands.

CHARLOTTE: Oh, don't sir, they're as black as I don't
know what.

DON JUAN: What are you talking about? They're beautiful.
Let me kiss them. Please.

CHARLOTTE: Oh, Sir, what an honour. If I'd known about this in advance, I could have given them a good scrub.

DON JUAN: Tell me, Charlotte, you're not married, are you?

CHARLOTTE: No, Sir, but I'm engaged to Pierrot, our neighbour's son.

DON JUAN: You mean you're going to waste yourself on some wretched peasant? That would be sacrilege, you're far too beautiful to bury yourself in a village. God knows that you deserve something better than that, and He has purposely led me here, so that I may prevent this marriage and do justice to you. I love you, Charlotte. All you have to do is say the word, and I'll take you away from this miserable place and raise you to the position you deserve. I know this love may seem rather sudden, but you must blame your great beauty for that, Charlotte, a quarter of an hour with you is like six months with someone else.

CHARLOTTE: Honestly, Sir, I don't know what to think when you talk like that. It's very nice what you say, and I want to believe it, really I do. But I've always been told that you should never believe a gentleman, because they're all liars, and all they're interested in is seducing people.

DON JUAN: I'm not that sort of person.

SGANARELLE: Perish the thought.

CHARLOTTE: Listen, Sir, it's no fun being seduced, you know. I'm only a poor girl, but I do have my honour, and I'd rather die than lose it.

DON JUAN: It would be really cowardly and despicable to take advantage of someone like you. Do you think

40

I would? I have a conscience, you know. I love you, Charlotte, sincerely and honourably. It's the truth - I intend to marry you, what greater proof can you ask? I'm ready whenever you like; and I take this man here as a witness to my promise.

ANARELLE: Don't worry. He means it. He'll marry you all right.

N JUAN: Oh, Charlotte, I can see that you don't know me yet. You're very wrong to judge me by other people's standards. I know there are cheats and un-scrupulous seducers in the world, but you mustn't think I'm one of them, you mustn't doubt my sin-cerity. But then, your beauty is your safeguard, you know. People who look like you don't have to worry about that sort of thing; believe me, no-one's going to take advantage of you; as for me, I'd kill myself on my sword rather than think of betraying you.

ARLOTTE: Oh, God, I don't know whether you're telling the truth or not; but it sounds so nice, I believe you.

N JUAN: You're right to. The promise I made still stands. Will you accept it and agree to marry me?

ARLOTTE: Yes, all right, providing my auntie doesn't mind.

N JUAN: Give me your hand, Charlotte, show me that you don't mind.

ARLOTTE: One thing, Sir, please don't deceive me, please. It'd be an awful thing to do, seeing as I trust you so much.

N JUAN: It doesn't sound as if you do. What do you want me to do? Shall I swear a solemn oath. May God ...

CHARLOTTE: Oh, dear, no need to do that, I believe
   you.
DON JUAN: Then just give me a little kiss to show me
   you mean it.
CHARLOTTE: Oh, Sir, please, let's wait till we're
   married; then I'll kiss you as much as you like.
DON JUAN: All right, Charlotte, whatever you like; ju
   give me your hand, and let me show you how I feel

SCENE THREE

DON JUAN, SGANARELLE, PIERROT, CHARLOT

PIERROT: (pushing DON JUAN away) Just a minute sir,
   steady on, will you. You'd better not get so worked
   up, you'll have a stroke or something.
DON JUAN: (pushes PIERROT roughly) What's this
   buffoon think he's doing?
PIERROT:(gets between DON JUAN and CHARLOTTE)
   Now, look here, just stop that, keep your hands off
   my fiancée.
DON JUAN: (pushes him again) Do you have to make suc
   a noise?
PIERROT: Ey, stop pushing me around.
CHARLOTTE: (takes PIERROT'S arm) Let him be,
   Pierrot.
PIERROT: What d'you mean, let him be? Why should I?
DON JUAN: Ah!
PIERROT: Just because you've got money, you think you
   can go touching up our women in front of us. Go and
   touch up your own.
42

N JUAN: What?

(He slaps PIERROT.)

PIERROT: Oy, don't hit me.

(Another slap)

Ow, Christ.

(Another)

Bluddyell.

(Another)

It's not very nice, hitting people, specially when
they've just saved you from drowning.

CHARLOTTE: Don't get angry, Pierrot.

PIERROT: I want to get angry. How dare you let him
carry on with you like that?

CHARLOTTE: It's not what you think, Pierrot. This
gentleman wants to marry me, there's no point in
getting all upset about it.

PIERROT: What do you mean? You're engaged to me.

CHARLOTTE: That doesn't make any difference, Pierrot,
he doesn't mind. If you love me, you ought to be
pleased I'm going up in the world.

PIERROT: Pleased? I'd rather see you dead than married
to someone else.

CHARLOTTE: Come on, Pierrot, don't be like that.
Look, I'll see you right when I'm married, you can
deliver butter and cheese to us, we'll be your best
customers.

PIERROT: I wouldn't deliver you the time of day, if you
paid me double for it. So you've given in to him,
have you? Jesus, if I'd known this was going to
happen, I'd have thought twice about fishing him out
of the water. In fact I'd have very likely fetched
his head a wallop with my oar.

N JUAN: (making to hit PIERROT) What's that you say?

43

PIERROT: (hiding behind CHARLOTTE) You don't scare ⟩
DON JUAN: Then come here.
PIERROT: (dodging him) I will in a minute!
DON JUAN: (chasing him) Come on then.
PIERROT: (hiding behind CHARLOTTE again) Don't yo
try anything with me!
DON JUAN: Ah!
SGANARELLE: Oh, leave him alone, sir, poor wretch
It's not fair to hit him. (to PIERROT, pushing in
between him and DON JUAN) Listen, lad, just go
away and don't say any more.
PIERROT: (pushing SGANARELLE aside and confronti
DON JUAN) What do you mean, don't say any more?
DON JUAN: I'll teach you.
(He swipes at PIERROT who ducks, so that he hits
SGANARELLE.)
SGANARELLE: (to PIERROT) You miserable idiot!
DON JUAN: (to SGANARELLE) The wages of virtue.
PIERROT: I'm going to tell your aunt about this.
(He exits.)
DON JUAN: At last. You're going to make me the happie
man in the world, and I wouldn't trade my happiness
for anything. What pleasures we shall see when
you're my wife ...

SCENE FOUR

DON JUAN, SGANARELLE, CHARLOTTE,
MATHURINE

SGANARELLE: (seeing MATHURINE) Whoops.
MATHURINE: (to DON JUAN) Now now, sir, what are
44

you doing with Charlotte. Not talking about love to
her as well, I hope.

N JUAN: (aside to MATHURINE) No, no, quite the
contrary. She seems to want me to marry her, I was
just explaining to her that I'm engaged to you.

ARLOTTE: (to DON JUAN) What's she after?

N JUAN: (aside to CHARLOTTE) She wanted me to
marry her, seeing me talking to you has made her
jealous; I told her it was you I wanted.

THURINE: Charlotte ...

N JUAN: (aside to MATHURINE) It's useless saying
anything, now she's got the idea into her head.

ARLOTTE: Look here, Mathurine ...

N JUAN: (aside to CHARLOTTE) There's no point in
talking to her, she's got such an imagination.

THURINE: Is there ...?

N JUAN: (aside to MATHURINE) It's impossible to
make her see reason.

ARLOTTE: I'd like to ...

N JUAN: (aside to CHARLOTTE) She's incredibly
obstinate.

THURINE: Well, I ...

N JUAN: (aside to MATHURINE) Don't talk to her,
she's mad.

ARLOTTE: I think ...

N JUAN: (aside to CHARLOTTE) Ignore her, she's
delirious.

THURINE: No, no, I must talk to her.

ARLOTTE: We've got to sort this out.

THURINE: What ...?

N JUAN: (aside to MATHURINE) I bet you she says
I've promised to marry her.

ARLOTTE: I ...

45

DON JUAN: (aside to CHARLOTTE) What's the betting she'll claim I proposed to her?

MATHURINE: Listen, Charlotte, you shouldn't poke your nose into other people's affairs, it's not right

CHARLOTTE: You got no right to be jealous if the gentleman wants to talk to me.

MATHURINE: He saw me first.

CHARLOTTE: He may have seen you first, but he saw second and he promised to marry me.

DON JUAN: (aside to MATHURINE) What did I tell you?

MATHURINE: (to CHARLOTTE) I beg your pardon, it's not you he promised to marry, it's me.

DON JUAN: (aside to CHARLOTTE) I guessed as much.

CHARLOTTE: You're talking through your hat: it's me

MATHURINE: I suppose you think that's funny: it's me.

CHARLOTTE: There he is, ask him if I'm wrong.

MATHURINE: See if he contradicts me.

CHARLOTTE: Did you promise to marry her, sir?

DON JUAN: (aside to CHARLOTTE) You're making fun me.

MATHURINE: Is it true you proposed to her, sir?

DON JUAN: (aside to MATHURINE) How can you think i

CHARLOTTE: See, she won't be told.

DON JUAN: (aside to CHARLOTTE) Never mind her.

MATHURINE: She still keeps on about it.

DON JUAN: (aside to MATHURINE) Let her.

CHARLOTTE: No, we've got to know the truth.

MATHURINE: It's got to be settled.

CHARLOTTE: Yes, Mathurine, I want you to get what's coming to you.

MATHURINE: Yes, Charlotte, it's time you were taken down a peg.

CHARLOTTE: Please sort this out, Sir.

THURINE: Let's get it over, Sir.

ARLOTTE: (to MATHURINE) You'll see.

THURINE: (to CHARLOTTE) So will you.

ARLOTTE: (to DON JUAN) Come on.

THURINE: (to DON JUAN) Tell us.

N JUAN: (embarrassed) What can I say? Both of you maintain I've promised to marry you. You know what the situation is, need I say more? Why force me to repeat myself? One of you is in a superior position, one of you knows I've given my word, so as long as I keep to it, why should you worry? In any case, there's no point in endlessly discussing it, actions speak louder than words, and ... er ... the end justifies the means. There you are, I hope that settles it, and when I do get married, we'll see which of you was right. (aside to MATHURINE) Let her think what she likes. (aside to CHARLOTTE) It's all in her imagination. (aside to MATHURINE) I adore you. (aside to CHARLOTTE) I'm yours. (aside to MATHURINE) Your beauty puts them all to shame. (aside to CHARLOTTE) You are perfection. Now. there's something I have to see to. I'll be back in about a quarter of an hour.
(Exits.)

ARLOTTE: See.

THURINE: What?

ARLOTTE: It's me he loves.

THURINE: Maybe, but it's me he's going to marry.

ANARELLE: You poor girls. I'm sorry for you, I can't bear to see you heading for disaster. Look, let me give you a piece of advice: don't believe all the stories you're told, go home now and stay there.

N JUAN: (returning) Sganarelle?

SGANARELLE: He's got no morals; all he wants to do
is to take advantage of you, that's all he ever want
he'll marry anything in skirts, that's ... (he sees
DON JUAN) ... all lies, of course, don't believe
anyone who tells you that. He wouldn't marry anything in skirts, he's got more morals than he knows
what to do with, and he's never taken advantage of
anybody. Oh, fancy, there he is, why don't you ask
him?

DON JUAN: Yes.

SGANARELLE: The world is full of liars, sir. I thought
I'd get in first and warn them not to believe anything
bad they might hear about you.

DON JUAN: Sganarelle!

SGANARELLE: Oh, yes, I guarantee he's a man of
honour.

  √ (DON JUAN bears down on him.)
Terrible liars, some people.

SCENE FIVE

DON JUAN, SGANARELLE, CHARLOTTE,
MATHURINE, LA RAMEE

LA RAMEE: Sir, I've come to warn you. You mustn't
stay here.

DON JUAN: What?

LA RAMEE: There are ten mounted men looking for you
they'll be here any minute. I don't know how they
managed to follow you here, but I just found out
about it from some peasant. They described you and

asked him if he'd seen you. I think the sooner you
get out of here, the better.

N JUAN: Right. (to CHARLOTTE and MATHURINE)
Urgent business, I'm afraid. Please remember my
promise. You'll hear from me before tomorrow
evening. (to SGANARELLE) Come on.

AN ARELLE: Erm ... do you want me to come with
you, sir?

N JUAN: Yes.

ANARELLE: Are you sure you wouldn't rather I
stayed behind and kept an eye on ...

N JUAN: Will you get a move on!

ANARELLE: If you insist.

(They exit.)

ACT THREE

SCENE ONE

DON JUAN less conspicuously dressed, SGANA-
RELLE disguised as a doctor

SGANARELLE: I feel happier like this.

DON JUAN: You look grotesque. Wherever did you dig u
that thing?

SGANARELLE: The pawnshop. It cost quite a lot, it
belongs to an old doctor. People respect you much
more if you wear something like this. Do you know,
since I got it, about five or six people have come up
to me for medical advice.

DON JUAN: And did you tell them you knew nothing abou
it?

SGANARELLE: No, of course not. I don't want to let
down the profession, do I? I made my diagnosis and
gave them all prescriptions.

DON JUAN: What for?

SGANARELLE: I don't know what for, whatever came int
my head at the time. It'd be a laugh if they got bette
wouldn't it, and came back to thank me.

DON JUAN: Why not? There's no reason you should do
worse than any other doctor. They're no more
responsible for cures than you are, it's all a lot of
mumbo-jumbo. All they do is cash in on the odd
fluke success, and if any of your patients come
through, why shouldn't you exploit their happiness
and take the credit for an entirely fortuitous

natural cure.

SGANARELLE: Don't you believe in medicine, either?

DON JUAN: One of man's greatest follies.

SGANARELLE: Don't you believe in sennapods? Or cassia? Don't you believe in emetic wine?

DON JUAN: Why should I?

SGANARELLE: An unbeliever. Haven't you heard about emetic wine, even the most sceptical people have been converted by the miracles it achieves. Only about three weeks ago I heard the most fantastic story about it.

DON JUAN: What?

SGANARELLE: Well, there was this man who'd been on the point of death for six days. They were at a loss, they'd tried everything and nothing worked. Finally, they decided to try emetic wine.

DON JUAN: And he got better, did he?

SGANARELLE: No, no, he died.

DON JUAN: A miracle.

SGANARELLE: No, look, he'd been trying to die for six whole days, and that did the trick straight away. Don't you think that's impressive?

DON JUAN: Very.

SGANARELLE: Oh, well, don't let's talk about medicine, you obviously don't believe in it, let's talk about something else. It's good for me, wearing this, makes me feel like arguing with you. I mean, I know you don't allow me to criticize you, but you don't mind a little debate, do you?

DON JUAN: No.

SGANARELLE: I want to know some of your opinions. Is it possible that you don't believe in God?

DON JUAN: Don't let's discuss that.

SGANARELLE: You mean you don't. What about Hell?

DON JUAN: What?

SGANARELLE: No Hell. What about the Devil, then?

DON JUAN: (sarcastically) Oh, yes.

SGANARELLE: All right then, don't you believe in the next life?

(DON JUAN laughs)

I can see I'm going to have trouble converting you. Next thing you'll be telling me you don't believe in ghosts, either.

DON JUAN: Don't be ridiculous.

SGANARELLE: Now that really does annoy me. I mean, whatever else they may think, everyone knows that ghosts exist. Look, you must believe in something. Don't you?

DON JUAN: Yes.

SGANARELLE: What?

DON JUAN: I believe that two and two are four, Sganarelle, and that four and four are eight.

SGANARELLE: Oh, that's very good. You believe in arithmetic. I must say, people have some funny ideas. Doesn't seem to matter how much you've studied, you don't come out any the wiser. Listen, sir, I haven't studied like you have, thank God, and no-one could ever claim to have taught me anything; but I can see things clearer than any book, because I've got a bit of common sense, a bit of judgment, and I can see that this world didn't just grow overnight like ... like a mushroom. Tell me who do you think made these trees, and rocks, and earth, and sky? Do you think they just happened? And what about you? There you are standing there. But you wouldn't be if your father hadn't made your

mother pregnant, would you? Look at the way man
is put together. Isn't it wonderful, all those intricate
components depending on one another? These nerves,
these bones, these veins, these arteries, these ...
this heart, these lungs, this liver and ... and all the
other ingredients which are ... which ... Oh, for
God's sake, come on, interrupt me. How can I
debate if you don't interrupt me? You're not saying
anything on purpose, it's very cruel, just letting me
rattle on like that ...

N JUAN: I'm waiting for you to come to the point.

ANARELLE: The point is, that whatever you may
say, there's some wonderful quality in man, that
can't be accounted for by science. Don't you think
it's a miracle that I'm standing here, thinking
hundreds of different thoughts at the same time,
making my body do whatever I want it to? See, I
can clap my hands, raise my arms, lift up my eyes
to Heaven, lower my head, move my feet, turn left,
right, forwards, backwards, spin round ... (He
falls over.)

N JUAN: I am unimpressed by your reasoning.

ANARELLE: Hell, I don't know why I waste my time
arguing with you. Believe what you like: it's not my
problem if you're damned.

N JUAN: Where are we, Sganarelle? Give that man
over there a shout, will you, and ask him how we
get out of here.

ANARELLE: Hey, you! Yes, you. Can you spare us
a minute, friend?

SCENE TWO

DON JUAN, SGANARELLE, BEGGAR

SGANARELLE: Can you tell us how to get to the town?

BEGGAR: All you have to do is follow this path and turn right when you get out of the forest. But be careful I warn you, recently there's been a lot of thieves in this area.

DON JUAN: It's very kind of you, my friend, thank you very much.

BEGGAR: If you'd like to make a contribution, sir ...

DON JUAN: Oh, I see, you weren't just warning us out of the kindness of your heart.

BEGGAR: I'm a poor man, sir. I've been a hermit for ten years, living in the woods. I'll pray for your prosperity, sir.

DON JUAN: Never mind me, I should pray for some new clothes, if I were you.

SGANARELLE: I can see you don't know this gentleman. All he believes in is that two and two are four, and four and four are eight.

DON JUAN: What do you do here in the forest?

BEGGAR: I spend all day praying for those kind people who give me something.

DON JUAN: Do well, do you?

BEGGAR: I'm afraid not, sir. I live in the most abject poverty.

DON JUAN: I don't believe it. Praying all day, you must be making a fortune.

BEGGAR: I promise you, sir, more often than not, I haven't even got a crust of bread to live on.

DON JUAN: Curious. Not much percentage in it then, is there? Now I'm going to give you a gold sovereign but I want you to do one thing for me. Blaspheme.

GGAR: Oh, no, sir I couldn't. It's a mortal sin.

N JUAN: It's entirely up to you. Do you want a gold
sovereign or not? Here's one, look. I'll give it to you
in return for a blasphemy. So let's hear you.

GGAR: Sir ...

N JUAN: You won't get it otherwise.

ANARELLE: Go on, just a little blasphemy, there's no
harm in it.

N JUAN: Take it, go on, take it: just blaspheme.

GGAR: No, sir, I'd rather starve.

N JUAN: Here you are, then, I give it to you for the
love of humanity. What's going on over there? Three
against one? It's not a fair fight, we can't allow
that!

SCENE THREE

DON JUAN, DON CARLOS, SGANARELLE

ANARELLE: He's mad. Leave well alone, I say. Wait
a minute... my God, it's worked, they're running away.

N CARLOS: (sword in hand) Thank you. Your help was
invaluable. It was most generous of you, sir, I ...

N JUAN: (sheathing his sword) I did nothing which
you would not have done in my place. It's a question
of honour. Not to have helped you against those
cowards would have been the same as helping them.
How did you fall into their hands?

N CARLOS: I've lost my brother and our party. I
was looking for them when those thieves attacked

55

me, and killed my horse. If it hadn't been for you,
they'd have done the same to me.

DON JUAN: Are you heading for the town?

DON CARLOS: In that direction, yes. At the moment my
brother and I are searching the countryside. It's
one of those unfortunate cases in which one's
honour forces one to ruin oneself: if we aren't
killed, the best we can hope for is exile.

DON JUAN: Would it be indiscreet to ask the details?

DON CARLOS: Well, I don't suppose it will be a secret
much longer, and once it gets out, I expect we'll
want as many people to know about it as possible,
so we can show we're defending our honour. Our
sister was seduced and kidnapped from a convent
by a man called Don Juan Tenorio, son of Don Louis
Tenorio. We've been after him for some days, and
today we almost traced him; but he seems to have
given us the slip again.

DON JUAN: Do you know this man, erm, Don Juan, do
you know him?

DON CARLOS: I don't, no. I've never met him. But my
brother's described him to me, he hasn't a very
good reputation, he's the kind of man who ...

DON JUAN: Say no more, please. I know the man
slightly, and I'm afraid I couldn't allow myself to le
you speak ill of him.

DON CARLOS: My dear sir, since it would be impossib
for me to speak anything but ill of him, I'd rather
not say anything at all, for your sake, that's the
least I can do, after all you have just saved my life
But however friendly you are with him, I hope
you're not going to condone his behaviour, I hope
you don't think it strange of us to want our revenge.

DON JUAN: On the contrary I'll do anything I can to help you. I am friendly with Don Juan, and there's not very much I can do about that. But he certainly shouldn't be allowed to get away with a crime like that, and I can undertake to make him give you satisfaction for it.

DON CARLOS: What kind of satisfaction?

DON JUAN: Whatever kind you and your brother are hoping for. So you can save yourself the trouble of going on looking for Don Juan: I guarantee to produce him wherever and whenever you would like to see him.

DON CARLOS: Well, sir, to those of us who've suffered at his hands, that's a very comforting thought. But after all you've done for me, I would find it very painful if you were to fight on his side.

DON JUAN: Unfortunately, Don Juan is such a close friend of mine, that if he were to fight, I couldn't very well avoid fighting with him.

DON CARLOS: It seems very cruel of Fate to make me owe my life to a friend of Don Juan ...

SCENE FOUR

DON ALONSO and THREE FOLLOWERS, DON CARLOS, DON JUAN, SGANARELLE

DON ALONSO: Water the horses, will you, and bring them on after us. I'm going to go on ahead a bit on foot. Good God, is that my brother? What are you doing here, talking to our mortal enemy?

DON CARLOS: Mortal enemy?

DON JUAN: (stepping back three paces and putting his hand defiantly on his sword hilt) I am Don Juan, yes, and I'm not going to deny my name just because I'm outnumbered.

DON ALONSO: (putting his hand to his sword) You traitor, I'll kill you ...
(SGANARELLE runs off to hide.)

DON CARLOS: No, stop! He saved my life, and if he hadn't helped me, I would have been killed by thieves.

DON ALONSO: What difference does that make? Help from an enemy should be treated only with indifference; to be grateful to him is absurd. Since your honour is infinitely more precious than your life, if you owe your life to the man who has stolen your honour, you owe him nothing.

DON CARLOS: I know the distinction a gentleman must always make between honour and life, Alonso. My gratitude has in no way affected my desire for vengeance. But I think I should be allowed to pay back my debt to him here and now, and give him the life I owe him, so that he can enjoy a reward for his good deed. For a few days.

DON ALONSO: No, if you postpone our revenge, you're risking our whole cause, we may never get another chance like this. It's a heaven-sent opportunity, and it's up to us to make the most of it. And if you don't want to take part, all you have to do is move away and leave it all to me.

DON CARLOS: Please, Alonso...

DON ALONSO: It's no use arguing with me, I'm going to kill him.

CARLOS: Now stop this, Alonso, I'm warning
you. I will not allow any attack to be made on him, I
don't care who makes it, I swear to God I'll defend
him with my life. So, if you want to fight you'd
better start with me.

ALONSO: You mean to say you'd fight on our
enemy's side against me?

CARLOS: I think we should be masters of our
feelings, Alonso, I think our courage should be
reasoned, not violent. I don't think we should let
ourselves give way to blind rage. I don't want to be
in the position of owing something to my enemy, the
first thing I must do is repay my debt. I hardly
think a little delay is going to diminish our revenge.
On the contrary, people will admire us even more,
if they know we passed up this opportunity.

ALONSO: I think it's feeble and short-sighted of
you to compromise our honour because of some
imaginary debt. It's a ridiculous idea!

CARLOS: There's no need to upset yourself,
Alonso. If I'm making a mistake, I shall know
exactly how to put it right, I take full responsibility
for safeguarding our honour, I know what it entails.
Don Juan, as you can see, I've made it my business
to return the favour I owe you. I'm sure it will
come as no surprise to you, if I say that I attach
equal importance to all my debts, and I'm just as
determined to pay back your injuries as I was to
reward your good deed. You've committed a very
great offence against me, you must know that, and I
leave you to judge how the matter can best be
settled: peacefully or with violence and blood. In
any case, whatever you decide, you gave me your

word I would get satisfaction from Don Juan: please keep your promise, and remember that from now on my only debt is to my honour.

DON JUAN: I've made no demands on you. And I always keep my promises.

DON CARLOS: Come with me, Alonso. A little self-restraint never harmed anyone.

SCENE FIVE

DON JUAN, SGANARELLE

DON JUAN: Hey! Sganarelle!

SGANARELLE: (appearing from his hiding-place) What can I do for you, sir?

DON JUAN: You wretch. What do you mean by hiding when I'm attacked?

SGANARELLE: No, no, I wasn't hiding, no, er ... I had to ... erm ... I was just over there. I think this doctor's outfit must act as some sort of laxative works better than a dose of salts.

DON JUAN: You abject buffoon. You might at least have thought up some slightly less repulsive excuse for your cowardice. Do you know whose life I just saved?

SGANARELLE: No. Should I?

DON JUAN: One of Elvira's brothers.

SGANARELLE: You what?

DON JUAN: He seemed a reasonable enough man, he behaved rather well, I'm sorry to have him as an enemy.

SGANARELLE: It'd be easy enough for you to sort
things out amicably if you wanted to.

DON JUAN: Yes, I know; but that passion I had for
Elvira, it's all drained away, it's no good, I don't
feel like going back to her. You know I like freedom
in love, I couldn't let my feelings be confined in
four walls. My natural inclination is to go after
everything that attracts me, I must have told you
that a hundred times. My heart belongs to every
beautiful woman, and it's up to them to take it one
by one, and keep it as long as they can. That's a
very imposing building through those trees there. Do
you know what it is?

SGANARELLE: Don't you?

DON JUAN: No. No, I don't.

SGANARELLE: You remember the Commander? That's
the tomb he was having built for himself when you
killed him.

DON JUAN: Oh, yes! I didn't know it was round here.
I've heard the most wonderful things about it,
especially about the Commander's statue. Let's go
and have a look.

SGANARELLE: No, sir, don't.

DON JUAN: Why not?

SGANARELLE: Well, it's not polite to go and look at a
man you've killed.

DON JUAN: On the contrary, what could be more polite
than to pay him a courtesy call. I'm sure he'll be
delighted, any gentleman would. Come on, follow me.
(The tomb opens to reveal a superb mausoleum and
the statue of the Commander.)

SGANARELLE: Isn't that beautiful? Beautiful statues.
Beautiful marble. Beautiful pillars. Isn't it

61

beautiful? What do you think, sir?

DON JUAN: I think you couldn't find a more ludicrous
example of the ambition of a corpse. What amazes
me is that a man who spent his life in a relatively
simple house should want such magnificent
surroundings to rot in.

SGANARELLE: There's the Commander's statue.

DON JUAN: My God, he's all got up like a Roman emperor

SGANARELLE: Look at that, sir, isn't it well done?
It's so lifelike, he looks as if he's about to say
something. I wouldn't like the way he's looking at
us, if I was by myself. I don't think he's very
pleased to see us.

DON JUAN: I can't think why, he should be honoured.
Ask him to come and have dinner with me.

SGANARELLE: I don't think dinner would do him much
good.

DON JUAN: Go on, ask him.

SGANARELLE: You're joking. Aren't you? I can't go
talking to a statue, it'll think I'm mad.

DON JUAN: Do what you're told.

SGANARELLE: It's ridiculous. Erm, Commander, er
Your Excellency, I know this sounds stupid ... I
can't stop laughing but my master's insisted I do it.
Your Excellency, my master, Don Juan, invites
you to do him the honour of having dinner with him.
(The STATUE nods.)
Ah!

DON JUAN: What? What is it? Tell me. Come on, say
something.

SGANARELLE: (nodding in imitation of the statue) The
statue ...

DON JUAN: Well? Go on, you fool, what about it?

62

ANARELLE: What I mean is the statue ...

JUAN: Well? What about the statue? If you don't
tell me, I'll ...

ANARELLE: The statue nodded.

JUAN: Don't be absurd.

ANARELLE: It did, it nodded, I tell you. True as I
stand here. Go and ask it yourself if you don't
believe me. Perhaps ...

JUAN: Come here, you halfwit, come on. I'll show
you what a coward you are. Watch this. Your
Excellency, would you care to come and have dinner
with me?

(The STATUE nods again.)

ANARELLE: I wouldn't have missed that for anything.
Well? Sir?

JUAN: Come on, let's get out of here.

ANARELLE: So much for unbelievers.

63

ACT FOUR

SCENE ONE

DON JUAN, SGANARELLE

DON JUAN: Well, whatever it was, never mind, it
doesn't matter. Probably a trick of the light or a
mirage or something.

SGANARELLE: Now, sir, don't try to deny it, we both
saw it, right in front of our very eyes. There's
no way you can get round it, the statue nodded. If
you ask me it was a miracle, a warning to you from
Heaven, because your life is such a scandal, it wa
to warn you to ...

DON JUAN: Look. If I have to listen to any more of you
crass moralizing, if I hear one more word from yo
about it, I'm going to call someone, fetch in a whip
have three or four people hold you down, and give
you a thousand lashes. Now is that quite understoo

SGANARELLE: Yes, sir, absolutely, sir, couldn't be
clearer. That's what I like about you, sir, you
never beat about the bush. You put things so lucid

DON JUAN: I want dinner now, as soon as possible.
Fetch me a chair, will you, boy?

SCENE TWO

DON JUAN, LA VIOLETTE, SGANARELLE

VIOLETTE: There's a tradesman here, sir, a
Mr. Dimanche, asking to see you.

ANARELLE: Oh, good, that's all we needed, a
creditor. What's he think he's doing coming here for
his money? Didn't you tell him the Master was out?

VIOLETTE: Yes, I told him that, three-quarters of
an hour ago. But he didn't seem to believe me,
he's sitting down there waiting.

ANARELLE: Oh, well, let him wait, he can wait as
long as he likes.

N JUAN: No, send him up. It's a very bad policy,
hiding from your creditors. It's far better to give
them something, and I know how to send them away
perfectly happy without paying them a penny.

SCENE THREE

DON JUAN, MR. DIMANCHE, SGANARELLE,
SERVANTS

N JUAN: (with exaggerated courtesy) Ah, Mr.
Dimanche, come in! How lovely to see you, I've
just been giving my servants a lecture for not
letting you in straight away. What happened was I
gave instructions not to be disturbed - but of course
that doesn't apply to you, my door is always open
for you.

R. DIMANCHE: Much obliged, sir, I'm sure.

DON JUAN: (to his servants) I'll teach you to leave
      Mr. Dimanche hanging about in the ante-chamber,
      you idiots, it's time you found out who's who.
MR. DIMANCHE: Oh, that's nothing, sir, really, I ..
DON JUAN: (to MR. DIMANCHE) I don't know what
      they thought they were doing, Mr. Dimanche,
      telling you I wasn't in, they know you're one of my
      best friends.
MR. DIMANCHE: I'm at your service, sir. The reason
      I ...
DON JUAN: A chair for Mr. Dimanche, come on, hurry
      up.
MR. DIMANCHE: No, that's all right, sir, I'm quite
      all right.
DON JUAN: No, you're not. I want you to come and sit
      next to me.
MR. DIMANCHE: Please don't, there's no need to er .
DON JUAN: No, no, no, not a stool, an armchair.
MR. DIMANCHE: I hope you're not making fun of me,
      sir, I ...
DON JUAN: No, of course not, I know how much I owe
      you, I don't want you to be made to feel inferior in
      any way.
MR. DIMANCHE: Sir ...
DON JUAN: Do sit down.
MR. DIMANCHE: No, it's all right, sir, I only just
      want to have a word with you. I was wondering ...
DON JUAN: Come and sit here.
MR. DIMANCHE: No, I'm quite happy standing, sir. I
      came over to ...
DON JUAN: No, I won't listen to a word unless you sit
      down.
MR. DIMANCHE: Just as you like, sir. Now, I ...

N JUAN: Good Heavens, Mr. Dimanche, you are looking well.

. DIMANCHE: Well, it's very kind of you to say so, sir. What I wanted to ask was ...

N JUAN: Mind you, I always think you look very healthy: sparkling eyes, nice full lips and a bit of colour in your cheeks.

. DIMANCHE: I wonder if you'd mind ...

N JUAN: And your wife, erm, Mrs. Dimanche?

. DIMANCHE: Very well, sir.

N JUAN: Well, thank God for that, she's a very fine woman.

. DIMANCHE: She's at your service, sir, as I am. I thought I'd ...

N JUAN: And your little girl, Claudine, how's she?

. DIMANCHE: Very well indeed.

N JUAN: She's such a pretty little girl, I'm terribly fond of her.

. DIMANCHE: It's very kind of you to say so, sir. You erm I ...

N JUAN: And how's little Colin, is he still banging about with his drum?

. DIMANCHE: Yes, just the same, sir. I ...

N JUAN: What about your little dog Brusquet? Still growling and nipping all the customers' ankles, is he?

. DIMANCHE: Worse than ever, sir, we really don't know what to do with him.

N JUAN: Don't be surprised if I want to know all the latest news about your family, I find them so interesting.

. DIMANCHE: Well, I'm sure we're all very obliged to you, sir. I ...

DON JUAN: (stretching out a hand) Your hand,
    Mr. Dimanche. I hope you really are a friend of
    mine.

MR. DIMANCHE: I'm at your service, sir.

DON JUAN: And I am at yours.

MR. DIMANCHE: You're too kind, sir. I ...

DON JUAN: There's nothing I wouldn't do for you.

MR. DIMANCHE: Well, sir, that's very decent of you.

DON JUAN: And I say that without any ulterior motive,
    believe me.

MR. DIMANCHE: I'm sure I've done nothing to deserve
    your generosity. Anyway, sir ...

DON JUAN: Oh, come along, now, Mr. Dimanche, don't
    be so formal. Why don't you stay and have dinner
    with me?

MR. DIMANCHE: No, sir, I couldn't really, I have to
    be getting along in a minute, I ...

DON JUAN: (rising) Quick, a torch to show Mr. Dimanche
    out, come on. I want four or five of you to get your
    muskets, and escort him to the door.

MR. DIMANCHE: (rising in turn) It's not necessary, sir
    I can see myself out. There's just one thing ...
    (SGANARELLE quickly removes the chairs.)

DON JUAN: What? I want you to be looked after, I'm
    very concerned about you. After all, I owe a lot
    to you. I mean, quite apart from the money.

MR. DIMANCHE: Ah! Yes, well, sir ...

DON JUAN: It's not a thing I'm ashamed of, you know,
    I'm always telling people about it.

MR. DIMANCHE: Perhaps ...

DON JUAN: You'd like me to see you home myself,
    would you?

MR. DIMANCHE: Of course not, sir, I wouldn't dream

68

of it. It just ...

JUAN: Then come and say goodbye to me properly.
(He embraces him.) Now don't forget I'm at your
disposal, there's nothing in the world I wouldn't
do for you.

(Exit DON JUAN)

ANARELLE: You must admit he's very fond of you.

. DIMANCHE: He is. He was so polite and compli-
mentary, I never got a chance to ask him for the
money.

ANARELLE: Well, I can assure you there's no one
in this house who wouldn't lay down his life for you.
I wish something would happen to you, I wish someone
would try to smash your head in or something; then
you'd see ...

. DIMANCHE: Yes, yes, I'm sure. If you could just
have a word with him about my money, Sganarelle.

ANARELLE: Oh, don't worry about that. He'll pay
you all right.

. DIMANCHE: And you owe me something as well,
don't you, Sganarelle.

ANARELLE: Oh, don't let's talk about that.

. DIMANCHE: What? I ...

ANARELLE: I'm quite well aware of what I owe you.

. DIMANCHE: Well, then ...

ANARELLE: Come along, Mr. Dimanche, let me
show you out.

. DIMANCHE: What about the money? ...

ANARELLE: (taking MR. DIMANCHE by the arm)
Now you don't really mean that.

. DIMANCHE: I want ...

ANARELLE: (pulling at him) Uh, uh, uh.

. DIMANCHE: The thing is ...

SGANARELLE: (pushing him) Not worth bothering
about.

MR. DIMANCHE: But ...

SGANARELLE: (pushing him) Now then.

MR. DIMANCHE: I ...

SGANARELLE: (pushing him offstage) Now then, I said

SCENE FOUR

DON LOUIS, DON JUAN, LA VIOLETTE,
SGANARELLE

LA VIOLETTE: (to DON JUAN) Sir, your father is here

DON JUAN: Oh, that's wonderful, that's all I needed.

DON LOUIS: I can see I'm embarrassing you and that
you could have very well done without my visit. To
tell you the truth, the feeling is quite mutual. You
may be sick and tired of seeing me, but I'm just as
sick and tired of your behaviour. You don't know how
much I wanted a son: I prayed for one, constantly,
with the most passionate urgency. I must have worn
God out with my prayers, I thought a son would be
joy and consolation of my life, and you've caused me
nothing but misery and torment. Do you think it's
easy to make excuses for you all the time, how do you
suppose I feel about your continual outrages, you've
already exhausted the generosity of the King and
cancelled out whatever merit my services may have
won me in his eyes, and whatever prestige I may have
had among my friends. How can you be so contemp-
tible? Aren't you ashamed of not living up to your

70

position? Or perhaps you're proud of it, is that it?
When have you ever behaved like a gentleman? Do
you think it's enough to come from a noble family
and to have a name and a coat of arms, when you
live like a criminal? It isn't, there's no such thing
as aristocracy without virtue. We can only inherit
the glory of our ancestors if we force ourselves to
resemble them, and your ancestors wouldn't recognize you as their offspring. Don't think all their
achievements give you any privileges: on the
contrary their distinction simply accentuates your
disgrace, it's a torch lighting up the shamefulness
of your behaviour. Let me tell you something, an
aristocrat who lives badly is an unnatural monster,
the only title worth the name is virtue, the way you
behave is much more important than the name you
sign, and I'd have more respect for a burglar's son
if he were a man of honour, than I'd have for a king's
son who lived like you.

N JUAN: You'd be more comfortable if you were
sitting down.

N LOUIS: I don't want to sit down, you insolent
wretch, and I've said enough, although I can see
that nothing I've said has made the slightest
impression on you. But I'm warning you, what you've
done has destroyed my love for you, and sooner
than you think, I'm going to find a way to put a stop
to your excesses, I'm going to punish you and wipe
out the shame of having brought you into the world.
(He exits.)

SCENE FIVE

DON JUAN, SGANARELLE

DON JUAN: Why don't you hurry up and die, it's the best thing you could do. Everyone should have their turn, I hate to see fathers living as long as their sons. (He sinks into his armchair.)

SGANARELLE: That was wrong of you, sir.

DON JUAN: Wrong?

SGANARELLE: Sir ...

DON JUAN: (getting up) Wrong?

SGANARELLE: Yes sir, it was wrong of you to put up with it, you should have thrown him out. I've never seen anything so impertinent. A father coming and complaining to his son, telling him to behave better and remember his birth and live respectably and a of other stupid nonsense. How could a man who knows what life is all about, like you, be expected put up with that. I was just thinking how patient yo are. If it had been me, I'd have sent him packing long ago. (Aside) I ought to be ashamed of myself. never thought I'd come down to this.

DON JUAN: How much longer is dinner going to be?

SCENE SIX

DON JUAN, ELVIRA, RAGOTIN, SGANARELLE

RAGOTIN: Excuse me, sir, there's a lady in a veil
here who wants to speak to you.

DON JUAN: Who can that be?

SGANARELLE: We'll have to wait and see.

ELVIRA: Don't be surprised, Don Juan, to see me here
so late, wearing these clothes. I've come to see you
about something very important, there's no sense
in waiting, what I want to say to you has to be said
now. I'm not angry any more, you'll find I've
changed a great deal since I last saw you. I'm not
going to reproach you any more, I'm not going to
make any more threats, I've lost interest in revenge.
God has driven out all those feelings I had for you,
all those crude and shameful desires; all that's
left is a kind of disembodied affection, tenderness,
I still love you, but I feel detached, disinterested,
I'm concerned more about your welfare than anything
else.

DON JUAN: (to SGANARELLE) I do believe you're
crying.

SGANARELLE: Sorry.

ELVIRA: And it's my pure and perfect love for you
which has led me here, to bring you a warning from
Heaven and to try to pull you back from the edge of
the precipice. I know what sort of life you lead,
Don Juan, and God has chosen me to seek you out and
tell you that your crimes have exhausted His mercy
and that His terrible wrath is about to overwhelm
you. The only way you can save yourself is to
repent and if you leave it one more day, it may be

73

too late for you to escape the most dreadful punishment. We no longer have any sort of a relationship. I've decided to withdraw from the world completely; but it would cause me great pain in my retreat, if someone I once loved were to be struck down by God's justice, and if I could persuade you to avoid the appalling fate that's threatening you, it would make me wonderfully happy. Please, Don Juan, do me one last favour - don't refuse me your salvation, I beg you. If not for your own sake, for mine, spare me the cruel pain of seeing you sentenced to eternal damnation.

SGANARELLE: Poor woman!

ELVIRA: I loved you so much, nothing in the world has ever been as dear to me as you were. I forgot my duty because of you, I did everything for you, and the only reward I ask is that you change your way of life and escape your destruction. If you love me or if you love yourself, I beg you to save yourself. And if the tears of someone you once loved are not enough, I appeal to you in the name of whatever means most to you.

SGANARELLE: Heart of stone!

ELVIRA: That's all I wanted to say to you, I must go now.

DON JUAN: It's very late, my dear, why don't you stay? I'm sure we can manage to find a room for you somewhere.

ELVIRA: No, Don Juan, don't try to keep me here any longer.

DON JUAN: But I assure you, Madam, it would give me great pleasure if you were to stay.

ELVIRA: I said no, please don't waste time trying to persuade me. Let me go now and please don't insist

on taking me home either. Just think about whether
you can profit from my advice.

SCENE SEVEN

DON JUAN, SGANARELLE, SERVANTS

DON JUAN: Do you know something, I couldn't help
feeling for her, there was something rather novel
and bizarre about it, those slightly rumpled clothes,
that air of melancholy, the way she was crying. I
thought it was rather pleasant, it made the ashes
start to glow again.

SGANARELLE: You mean what she said had no effect
on you at all.

DON JUAN: Hurry up with the dinner.

SGANARELLE: Yes, sir.

DON JUAN: (sitting at the table) No, but Sganarelle, I
must think about turning over a new leaf.

SGANARELLE: You must, sir, yes.

DON JUAN: A new leaf, yes, my word, yes. Another
twenty or thirty years of this life and I must have
a serious think about it.

SGANARELLE: Oh, I see.

DON JUAN: What's that?

SGANARELLE: Nothing. Here's your dinner.
(He takes a piece of meat from one of the plates
being brought in and pops it in his mouth.)

DON JUAN: Something wrong with your cheek, is there?
Looks swollen to me. What's the matter with it?
Mm? Speak up.

SGANARELLE: Nothing.

DON JUAN: Let's have a look. Good heavens, it's a gum boil. It'll have to be lanced, quick, fetch me something sharp. Look, the poor fellow can hardly bear it, you can choke on an abscess like that. It's come to a head already ... Ah! You wretch!

SGANARELLE: No, I just wanted to make sure the cook hadn't put too much pepper or salt.

DON JUAN: Come on, sit down and eat. (I want you to do something for me after supper.) You look as if you're hungry.

SGANARELLE: (sitting at the table) I am, sir. I haven't eaten since this morning. Try some of this, it's very good indeed.

(As soon as SGANARELLE has filled his plate, a servant removes it.)

Hey, just a minute, my plate. If you don't mind, just a minute. Well, really, I've heard of quick service. I only wish you were as quick with the wine, La Violette.

(While the wine is being poured, SGANARELLE'S plate is removed again.)

DON JUAN: Who's that knocking?

SGANARELLE: Who the hell's that right in the middle of dinner?

DON JUAN: Don't let anyone in, I want to eat in peace.

SGANARELLE: I'll deal with it.

DON JUAN: (seeing SGANARELLE returning terrified) Well? Who is it?

SGANARELLE: (nodding his head like the statue) The .. it's the ...

DON JUAN: Let's go and see, it can't frighten me.

SGANARELLE: What am I doing to do?

SCENE EIGHT

DON JUAN, THE STATUE OF THE COMMANDER,
SGANARELLE, SERVANTS

The STATUE comes in and sits at the table.

DON JUAN: Come on, fetch a chair. Lay a place, hurry up. (to SGANARELLE) Sit down.

SGANARELLE: Not hungry any more, sir.

DON JUAN: Will you sit down! Some wine. Let's drink to the Commander's health, Sganarelle. Give him some wine.

SGANARELLE: Not thirsty, sir.

DON JUAN: Drink up, and then sing your song, give the Commander a treat.

SGANARELLE: Got a cold, sir.

DON JUAN: Never mind. Come on. And you accompany him, you others.

THE STATUE: That's enough, Don Juan. I invite you to come and have dinner with me tomorrow. Will you have the courage to?

DON JUAN: Certainly, I shall come alone - except for Sganarelle.

SGANARELLE: Er, ha, well, thank you, it's very kind, but I'm fasting tomorrow.

DON JUAN: (to SGANARELLE) Take the torch.

THE STATUE: We need no light, God shows the way.

ACT FIVE

SCENE ONE

DON JUAN, DON LOUIS, SGANARELLE

DON LOUIS: Well, my son, perhaps my prayers have
been heard in Heaven. Is it really true, what you
say? You're not deceiving me with false hopes, are
you? It's so sudden, are you sure it's a genuine
conversion?

DON JUAN: (hypocritically) Yes, I've turned my back o:
all my mistakes. Since last night I've become a
different man, all of a sudden there's been a chang
in me which will surprise everyone. God has touch
my soul and the scales have dropped from my eyes
to reveal the horror of my long blindness and the
criminal wickedness of my life. When I think of all
the abominations I have committed, I'm amazed that
God can have tolerated me for so long without
striking me down a dozen times over. But He has
not punished me, He has shown me His mercy - and
I intend to make the most of it by showing everyone
how radically my life has changed, and by atoning
for my scandalous behaviour until I have won back
His true forgiveness. That is what I shall work
towards: and I beg you, Sir, be kind enough to hel
me in my quest and choose someone who can act as
my guide and mentor along the paths of righteousne

DON LOUIS: Oh, my son, a father's love is easily

revived. All the pain you've caused me is already
forgotten. I admit, I'm quite bewildered, I feel like
crying for joy, all my prayers are answered. Kiss
me, my son, and persevere with this. I'm going
straight home to tell your mother the happy news
and to thank God for inspiring you with these holy
thoughts.

SCENE TWO

DON JUAN, SGANARELLE

SGANARELLE: Sir, I can't tell you how happy it makes
me to see you repent. I've been expecting it for a
long time now and thank God all my hopes have been
fulfilled.

DON JUAN: Buffoon.

SGANARELLE: What do you mean, buffoon?

DON JUAN: I suppose you believed all that, I suppose
you thought I meant what I said.

SGANARELLE: What? You aren't ... you're not ...
your ... What a man. What a man. What a man.

DON JUAN: No, I haven't changed at all, I'm still the
same as ever.

SGANARELLE: You're not taking any notice of the
Statue, a moving, talking statue, you don't find
that at all worrying?

DON JUAN: Well, I admit there's something about that I
don't completely understand: but whatever it is, I'm
not convinced by it, and I refuse to be intimidated.
And when I said I wanted to turn over a new leaf and

lead an exemplary life, it was pure expedience, a
plan I've worked out, a useful strategy, a disguise
I need to assume if I want to make use of my father
and protect myself from the various unfortunate
situations that are likely to arise. I'm taking you
into my confidence, Sganarelle, it's good to have
one person who understands how I feel and what my
real motives are.

SGANARELLE: You mean you don't believe in anything
and you're going to set yourself up as a man of
principle?

DON JUAN: Why shouldn't I? There are enough other
people doing the same thing, using the same mask t
deceive the world.

SGANARELLE: What a man. What a man.

DON JUAN: There's no disgrace in that nowadays.
Hypocrisy is a fashionable vice, and all fashionabl
vices count as virtues. Of all the characters one
can play today, the best is the man of principle,
the professional hypocrite holds all the advantages
Your pretence is always respected, and even if
you're found out, no one dares say a word against
you. Any other vice is liable to be condemned by
anybody who feels inclined to attack it; but hypocri
is a privileged vice, it can silence everyone and
remain serenely invulnerable. Once you put on the
mask, you become part of a kind of secret society,
and if anyone attacks you, he brings the whole ban
of you down on him. And you can always take in the
people who really are pious and who are known to
act in good faith, because if the disguise looks
realistic enough, they'll always fall into the trap a
support you blindly. I've seen so many men pick thi

method to buy back the scandals of their youth, and
use religion as a shield and respectability as a
licence to become the wickedest men in the world.
Even if people know what they're plotting, even if
they're recognized for what they are, it doesn't
matter, it still doesn't seem to damage their
reputation - all they need to see them through is a
bowed head, an ascetic sigh, and a bit of eyeball-
rolling. It's an excellent way to protect oneself and
I intend to make the most of it, I need some security.
I shan't give up my delightful way of life - but I shall
take care to be discreet and amuse myself stealthily.
And if I am ever caught out, I shan't have to lift a
finger, the secret society will look after me and
defend me against everything. In fact, it means I can
do whatever I like with impunity. I shall set myself
up as a moralist, pass judgment on everyone and take
a poor view of everyone except myself. If a man
commits the slightest impropriety, I shall never
forgive him, my hatred for him will be quite im-
placable. I shall become the vengeance of God, and
it'll be a useful pretext to stamp on my enemies,
I shall simply accuse them of impiety, and let loose
on them all those loud-mouthed bigots who will
attack them publicly, drown them in insults and use
their private authority to ruin them completely.
That's the way to profit from people's weaknesses.
That's the way an intelligent man makes the most
of contemporary vices.
SGANARELLE: Oh, my God, whatever next? Hypocrisy:
that's all you needed to round you off nicely,
that's the finishing touch. It's more than I can stand,
sir, I've got to say this, I can't help myself. Do

whatever you like to me, hit me, beat my head in, kill me if you like - but I must get this off my mind, as your faithful follower I have to say this to you. The fact is, sir, you can have too much of a good thing and be hoist with your own petard. And as that famous writer whose name escapes me once said: man lives in this world like the bird in its nest; the nest is at the top of the tree; to get to the top of the tree you must follow the paths of righteousness; righteousness speaks louder than pretty words; pretty words are heard at court; court is for the courtiers; the courtiers follow the fashion; fashion is a product of the imagination; imagination is a faculty of the soul; the soul is what gives us life; life ends in death; death makes us think of Heaven; Heaven is above the earth; the earth is not the sea; the sea is subject to storms; storms are a danger to shipping; a ship needs a good pilot; a good pilot is reliable; you can't rely on the young; the young should obey the old; the old like money; money makes you rich; the rich aren't poor; the poor are short of the necessary; necessity knows no law; if you have no law, you live like an animal; and that's why you're going to be damned right to Hell.

DON JUAN: Oh, you're very persuasive.

SGANARELLE: And if you don't mend your ways after that, on your own head be it.

SCENE THREE

DON CARLOS, DON JUAN, SGANARELLE

DON CARLOS: Ah, here you are, Don Juan, I'm glad
to have a chance to talk to you here rather than at
your house, to find out what your plans are. You
know it's my job to sort this thing out, you remember
I made myself responsible for it when we last met.
I won't deny that I'd be happier if we could arrive
at a friendly settlement, and I'd give anything to
be able to persuade you to confirm your marriage
to my sister in public.

DON JUAN: (hypocritically) I'd love to be able to do that
for you, I only wish I could; but alas it's not God's
will. He has inspired me and filled my mind with
the idea of reforming my life, so that my only
preoccupation is to renounce all my worldly attach-
ments, to put every kind of vanity behind me and to
hope that my way of life will be sufficiently austere
to make up for all the criminal excesses of my
blind, impetuous youth.

DON CARLOS: I can't see that your intention raises any
difficulties: if Heaven has inspired you with these
excellent principles, I see no reason why you
shouldn't follow them in the company of a legitimate
wife.

DON JUAN: I'm afraid it's impossible. Your sister has
made the very same plans. Our conversions were
simultaneous.

DON CARLOS: Her decision to go into retreat is not
satisfactory to us. It could easily be attributed to
your insulting behaviour towards her and towards
our family. Our honour demands that she should live

83

with you.

DON JUAN: It's impossible, I assure you. As far as I'm
concerned I'd like nothing better, in fact I even went
so far as to consult God on the subject this morning.
But I heard a voice which told me that I should banis
your sister from my thoughts, because with her I
should surely find no salvation.

DON CARLOS: Do you think we're going to let ourselves
be dazzled by these excuses?

DON JUAN: I must obey the voice of God.

DON CARLOS: You expect me to be taken in by this sort
of talk?

DON JUAN: It's God's will.

DON CARLOS: You seduce my sister from a convent and
then desert her ...

DON JUAN: God has ordained it thus.

DON CARLOS: ... and you expect my family to overlook
this stain on our honour.

DON JUAN: You must complain to God.

DON CARLOS: Will you not keep talking about God all
the time.

DON JUAN: That's the way God likes it.

DON CARLOS: That's quite enough, Don Juan, I
understand. This is neither the time nor the place to
deal with you, but before very long I shall know
where to find you.

DON JUAN: Do what you like. You know I'm not lacking
in courage and that I know how to use my sword whe
it's necessary. I shall very soon be using that little
side road which leads to the convent - but I must
emphasize that I have no desire to fight you whatsoever. God forbid. However if you attack me, we
shall see what happens.

N CARLOS: We shall, you're right, we shall see.

SCENE FOUR

DON JUAN, SGANARELLE

AN ARELLE: What sort of behaviour is that, sir?
Worse than the other. I preferred you the way you
were before. I was hoping you'd be saved; but now
I despair of you. God's put up with you up to now,
but He's not going to put up with this latest outrage.
N JUAN: Get on with you, God isn't as demanding as
you think. If every time anyone ...
AN ARELLE: (seeing the GHOST) God's speaking to
you, sir, it's a warning ...
N JUAN: If God wants me to understand what he's
saying, He'd do well to speak a little more clearly.

SCENE FIVE

DON JUAN, A GHOST IN THE FORM OF A VEILED
WOMAN, SGANARELLE

OST: Don Juan has only a few more seconds to profit
from God's mercy. If he does not repent here and
now, he is lost.
AN ARELLE: Do you hear, sir?
N JUAN: How dare you say that to me? I think I
recognize that voice.

SGANARELLE: It's a ghost, sir. You can tell by the
way it moves.

DON JUAN: I don't care if it's a ghost, a devil or a
pixie, I want to get hold of it.

✓ (The GHOST changes shape to represent time, with
its scythe.)

SGANARELLE: Oh, God! Did you see it change shape,
sir?

DON JUAN: No, nothing can frighten me, where's my
sword, I'll soon find out if it's flesh and bone.
(The GHOST vanishes as DON JUAN tries to strike
at it.)

SGANARELLE: Give up, sir, how much more proof do
you want, don't waste any more time, repent.

DON JUAN: No, no, whatever happens, it'll never be
said that I gave way and repented. Follow me.

SCENE SIX

THE STATUE, DON JUAN, SGANARELLE

THE STATUE: Stop, Don Juan. Yesterday you gave me
your word you would come and have dinner with me.

DON JUAN: Yes. Where shall we go?

THE STATUE: Give me your hand.

DON JUAN: Here you are.

THE STATUE: Don Juan, a hardened sinner can only
expect death, and if you reject God's mercy, all
that is left is His wrath.

DON JUAN: Oh, God! What's happening to me? I'm on
fire. I can't bear it. My whole body's burning up. A

(A great crash of thunder. DON JUAN is lit up by great flashes of lightning. The earth opens and swallows him up. Great flames leap out of the ground at the spot where he has disappeared.)

SGANARELLE: My wages, what about my wages? Now he's dead, I'm sure everyone's satisfied - the God he insulted, the laws he broke, the girls he seduced, the families he disgraced, the parents he outraged, the wives he perverted, the husbands he destroyed, everyone, they're all delighted. Except for me. I'm the only one who's unhappy. My wages. My wages. My wages.